Staffords
Churches and

on old picture postcards

Roy Lewis

1. St Dominic's Roman Catholic Church, Stone, was built in 1853-4 as part of the convent established by Mother Margaret Hallahan. She had faith in a growing congregation and encouraged the architect, Joseph Hanson, to build ambitiously. This 1910 postcard by Louis Dutton shows the rich thirteenth century style of the interior.

**Designed and Published by
Reflections of a Bygone Age,
Keyworth, Nottingham
1996**

ISBN 1 900138 06 9

£3.50

**Produced and Printed by
Print Rite, School Lane,
Stadhampton, Oxford**

Front cover:
St Chad's, Slindon, a little Victorian gem of a church, was built in 1894 by Basil Champneys at the expense of T.C.Salt, the Stafford banker, yet has a feel of the middle ages. Postcard published by E.J.Hurlstone of Eccleshall, and posted from there in July 1920.

Back cover (top):
The Tabernacle, Hanley, built in 1883 and closed in 1964, took its name from George Whitefield's chapel in London. It was the centre for Congregational work all over North Staffordshire and was once described as *"A nonconformist cathedral"*. Wrench postcard of 1906.

Back cover (bottom):
St Mary's, Stafford, was a royal free chapel and collegiate church until the sixteenth century. By the 1840's the medieval building was in decay and George Gilbert Scott was engaged to restore it - his first church restoration. In 1945 the churchyard, seen in this 1903 postcard by Hunt of Manchester, was levelled and became a Garden of Remembrance.

2. St Mary's, Tutbury, was originally part of a Norman Priory. When the Priory was dissolved in 1538, the building was rescued as the parish church. This 1914 postcard by J.S.Simnett shows both the impressive Norman west front and the south door with a boar hunt carved on the lintel.

3. This W.H.Smith & Son postcard of 1916 shows the nave of St Mary's, Tutbury. The pillars are all Norman but those with a quatrefoil section on the right are later than the round pillars further away. The apse at the end of the nave is a nineteenth century addition. Card posted at Burton-on-Trent.

Introduction

Staffordshire has a wide range of churches and chapels dating from Norman times to the present day. These have been a favourite subject for postcard publishers since the first picture postcards in 1894. For many years photographing church interiors demanded long exposures. The daughter of one Staffordshire photographer remembers how her father told her that she could run around while he photographed the church interior as long as she did not stand still long enough to appear on the negative. The need for a long exposure explains the absence of postcards showing people in church and the uneven quality of some real photographic cards.

Selecting 56 churches for inclusion in this book has been difficult and many buildings that I would have liked to include have had to be omitted through lack of space. I have tried to choose a cross-section of town and country churches, to include Nonconformist chapels and Roman Catholic churches as well as Parish churches, and to illustrate the rich variety of buildings used for religious purposes. A few of the churches are no longer standing and others have changed - especially interior fittings. Note, for example, how country churches were lit before the days of universal electricity. Lichfield Cathedral, and churches which are no longer in Staffordshire have been deliberately omitted.

The book is arranged in a broadly chronological sequence so that the reader is led from churches which retain Norman features at the beginning to examples of twentieth century buildings at the end.

When I was a boy before the war, wherever we went my father always took me on a tour of the local church, posing questions and pointing out features of interest. Today, regrettably, most churches are kept locked, except at service times, to prevent vandalism and theft. However, I hope readers will be encouraged to browse round churches wherever they go. Exteriors are always accessible and, for those with a real interest, keys can almost always be produced and often a well-informed guide comes with them.

Roy Lewis
March 1996

4. St Chad's Stafford, is the most complete Norman church in the county. This postcard, published by Valentine of Dundee, shows the chancel arch with its sumptuous zig-zag and two rows of beak heads as well as the Norman arcading with heavy round pillars and semi-circular arches.

5. St Peter's, Alstonfield, is an old church with Saxon fragments built into the walls. This postcard by R.& R.Bull of Ashbourne shows the Norman chancel arch in 1910. The chancel was rebuilt by Lawrence Berrisford in 1590 and the box pews, lectern and pulpit all date from the early seventeenth century.

6. St Chad's, Seighford, was built in the late twelfth century. Its Norman tower collapsed about 1610 damaging the south aisle, which was rebuilt in local red brick. This W.H.Smith & Son postcard shows the interior in the 1920s with the Norman chancel arch in the centre and another Norman arch on the left.

7. An unknown photographer posed these parishioners outside St Margaret's, Draycott-in-the-Moors, on a summer day in 1912. The tower is thirteenth century, the windows fourteenth century, and the whole restored in Victorian times. Visitors should not miss the Draycott family monuments in the north chapel.

8. This magnificent seven-foot high sandstone statue of Christ was found beneath the floor of St Mary's, Swynnerton, in 1811 and is now in the south chapel of the church. The origin of the thirteenth century statue is unknown although it has been suggested that it was once part of Lichfield Cathedral.

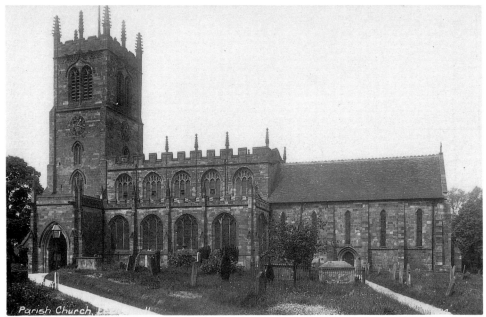

9. Eccleshall was the home of the Bishop of Lichfield until 1867 and the thirteenth century Holy Trinity Church was large enough to hold Bishops' functions in it. The chancel's lancet windows contrast with those of the fifteenth century clerestory and south aisle. Postcard by E.J.Hurlstone, 1913.

10. Penkridge was home to a college of ten priests under a Dean. At the height of their prosperity in the thirteenth century they built this red sandstone church dedicated to St Michael and All Angels, adding a tower and clerestory in the fourteenth and new windows in the sixteenth century. A 1936 Valentine postcard.

TAMWORTH CHURCH.

11. St Editha's Parish Church, Tamworth, was gutted by fire in 1345 and rebuilt by Dean Baldwin de Witney. The tower should have had a spire but danger of subsidence led to its omission except for the small base just visible on this 1905 postcard by W. Carrick.

THE CHANCEL. TAMWORTH CHURCH.

12. This 1930's postcard shows the spacious chancel of St Editha's, Tamworth. On the right is Norman masonry that survived the 1345 fire and on the left the north wall rebuilt by Baldwin de Witney. The effigies in the recesses include Sir John Ferrers (died 1512) and his two wives.

13. St Lawrence's, Rushton Spencer, stands on a hill outside the village. It has low seventeenth century walls, the date 1713 on its studded door, and a nineteenth century stone tiled roof with dormers. All this disguises a rare 600-year-old timber church that once had a thatched roof.

14. Inside St Lawrence's the massive oak piers and beams of the medieval church are clearly visible. In 1830 the floor was of packed earth. Oil lamps were still in use in 1920 when G.Hill of Leek published both the postcards on this page.

15. St Margaret's, Betley, is a very different timber-framed church. In the nave, timber arcades are supported by octagonal piers each cut from a single Spanish chestnut tree trunk. The medieval screen dividing the north chapel, on the left in this postcard by T.Warham, is also of Spanish chestnut.

16. All Saints', Dilhorne, is the only wholly octagonal church tower in Staffordshire. Its lower stage is thirteenth century and the upper stage late fourteenth or fifteenth century. The rest of the church is of similar dates except the aisles and clerestory added in 1819.

Giffard's Tombs, Brewood.

17. St Mary and St Chad's, Brewood, is a handsome building with four altar tombs of the Gifford family from nearby Chillington. This 1929 postcard by J.Wakefield shows the north side of the chancel with left to right, John (died1613) and his wife, and Sir Thomas (died 1560) with two wives and seventeen children.

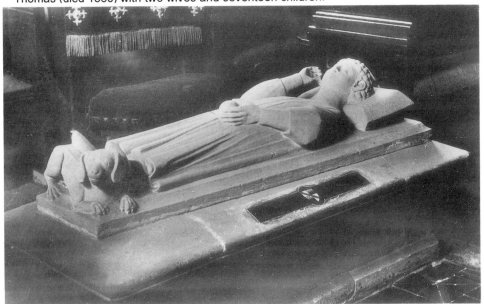

18. Visitors to St Peter's, Elford, should look for the fine effigies in the Stanley Chapel. This 1935 postcard from H.M.Griffiths shows the memorial to John Stanley, a youth who died about 1460 after being hit on the head by a tennis ball. He holds the ball in one hand and points to his head with the other.

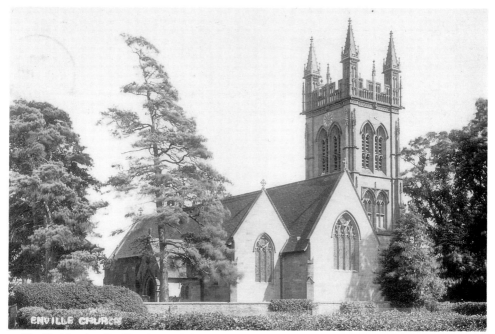

19. St Mary's, Enville, is a pink sandstone church of many dates. Inside are fine misericords and ancient stone figures. The church was rebuilt by Sir George Gilbert Scott who gave it the magnificent tower with its ornate pinnacles and battlements seen on this postcard sent from Cleobury Mortimer in June 1906.

20. St James', Barton-under-Needwood, was built as a chapel-of-ease by Dr John Taylor, chaplain to Henry VIII, whose career is described on shields in the nave. The building, consecrated in 1533, remains largely as built. The three-sided apse, seen on the right in this postcard by H.Simmonds, is unusual.

21. This William Shaw postcard of 1910 shows St Peter's, Broughton, built in 1633 as a private chapel for the Broughton family in a Gothic style already out of date. Inside, the original box pews and furniture remain, as well as stained glass that is older than the church.

22. The interior of St Mary's, Ingestre, retains its original carved oak screen with the Royal Arms of Charles II, its oak pulpit and plaster ceiling. It was also the first church in the county to be lit by electricity. This 1908 postcard by R.W.Dawson shows the original wrought-iron lighting standards still in use today, Card posted at Stafford and sent to Selby Park.

23. St Mary's, Ingestre, built for Walter Chetwynd of Ingestre Hall in 1676 in the style of Wren, is said to be the finest Renaissance church outside London. Unbelievably, this classical church was built less than 50 years after St Peter's on the opposite page. A 1930s Raphael Tuck postcard.

24. St Mary's, Patshull, a sandstone church in classical style, was designed by James Gibbs (who had built the nearby Hall) and consecrated in 1743. The tower was given a larger cupola in the 1870's to house a new peel of bells. The church is now officially redundant. A Wrench postcard, 1905.

Patshull Church   G.Miller Series

25. The interior of St Mary's, Patshull, is shown on this 1914 postcard by G.Miller. The square pillars on the left date from 1874, when Lord Dartmouth added a north aisle in memory of Bishop Lonsdale. The wrought iron screen (dated 1893) was a memorial to Lord Dartmouth himself.

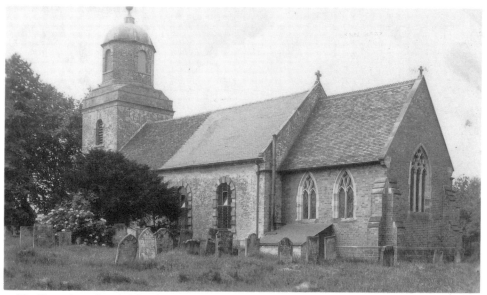

26. The charming brick church of St Peter at Marchington was built by Richard Trubshaw in 1742. In the nineteenth century the Victorians added a chancel (on the right in this 1925 postcard by Alfred McCann of Uttoxeter) in a Gothic style out of keeping with the rest of the church.

Ent.
Stationers' Hall.]

Armitage Pictorial Post Card.

[Date
As Postmark.

Bornfirmed at this Church

St. Nicholas Church, Mavesyn Ridware, Rugeley.

27. Much of the medieval church of St Nicholas, Mavesyn Ridware, was rebuilt in brick in 1782. This 1901 postcard shows the sharp contrast between the red brick nave and chancel and the medieval tower and north aisle. In the north aisle is an extraordinary collection of reliefs, incised slabs and tomb chests of the Mavesyn family.

28. After the Reformation, the medieval church attached to Burton Abbey became the parish church of Burton-on-Trent. By 1710 the roof was dangerous and the doors nailed up. The new church of St Modwen, seen on this 1922 postcard by Jackson & Co., was built in 1719-26 by Smith of Tettenhall.

29. The massive Tuscan columns supporting the roof galleries of St Modwen's can be seen on this 1904 Valentine's postcard. the pulpit, communion rail and chandelier (just visible in the chancel) are all of the same date as the church. Most pews were rented to individuals until 1962.

30. St John the Baptist Church at Lane End, Longton, was built of brick in 1792-5 in a classical style. The upper windows lit the galleries. The transepts, added in 1828, (on the right in this postcard by William Blake) show traces of Gothic influence. The church has now been demolished.

31. St Bartholomew's, Longnor, built in 1780, has no division between nave and chancel. In 1812 the church was heightened and additional windows inserted when the galleries were added. This R.& R.Bull postcard, showing the view towards the altar and eastern Venetian window, was taken from beneath the only gallery remaining in 1915.

32. St Michael's, Stone, rebuilt in the 1750s has been described as a *"a large formal preaching box"*. The message on this 1904 card reads, *"Went to the rector's daughter's wedding today. Quite a gay scene. The dress was beautiful but not a pretty face among 180 guests"*. It was posted from Stone to Nantwich.

Interior of St. Michael's Church, Stone.   *Photo. by P.C. Dutton, Stone.*

33. This 1920s postcard by P.C.Dutton of Stone shows the attractive interior of St Michael's, Stone, with its side galleries and eighteenth century box pews. The window in perpendicular Gothic style behind the altar was added when the chancel was rebuilt in the 1880s.

34. In 1814 the spire of St Mary's, Uttoxeter, was struck by lightning and masonry dislodged. The fourteenth-century church was already in poor repair and in 1828 was rebuilt in the same architectural style as the old church. This Valentine postcard shows the interior in 1905.

CATHOLIC CHURCH & LONDON ROAD, NEWCASTLE.

35. Holy Trinity Roman Catholic Church, Newcastle, has been described as *"a crazy effort"* and as *"the finest ornamental brickwork"*. The facade was created out of Staffordshire blue bricks by the Rev James Egan in 1833. A single window with brick tracery is surrounded by tiers of blank brick arcading. 1905 postcard by William Shaw.

36. As you approach Cheadle, the 200 foot spire of St Giles Roman Catholic Church attracts immediate attention. The church, built by Pugin in 1841-6, is one of the most perfect examples of the revival of Gothic architecture in the nineteenth century. Postcard by Jacob Lowndes, 1910.

37. Pugin also designed the interior of St Giles. This 1905 postcard by William Shaw shows the arcade with octagonal pillars and moulded arches. Everywhere is covered with ornate carving or rich colour.

38. St Gregory's Roman Catholic Church in Heathcote Road, Longton, was built by Pugin in 1868-9. The opulent ornaments and colourful stained glass of the sanctuary is clearly shown in this 1910 postcard by William Blake. The church, damaged by mining subsidence, had to be demolished in 1968.

39. The Church of the Holy Angels, Hoar Cross, is a church that must be seen. It was built in the 1870s by the Hon. Emily Meynell-Ingram in memory of her husband. The building and its sumptuous interior, seen on this McCann postcard, are George Bodley's imaginative interpretation of fourteenth century English Gothic.

The Altar Tomb
3471 Simnett MOST CLEAR CHURCH PHOTOGRAPHER
BURTON on TRENT

40. The focal point of the Church of the Holy Angels is the chancel and here, under a stone arch separating chancel from chantry chapel, is the tomb and white marble effigy of Hugo Francis Meynell-Ingram (died 1871) in whose memory the church was built. Postcard by J.S.Simnett of Burton-on-Trent.

41. This 1915 postcard by William Blake of Longton shows the nineteenth century Sutherland family monuments in the south chapel of St Mary and All Saints', Trentham. They include a statue of George, Duke of Sutherland; a recumbent effigy of Harriet, Duchess of Sutherland; and a medallion of Florence Chaplin.

SUTHERLAND ANCESTRAL MONUMENTS, TRENTHAM CHURCH. B66

42. St John the Baptist, Ashley, was rebuilt, except for the tower, in 1860. In 1910 the interior was refitted with screens, gilded reredos, chandeliers, etc., all designed by Cecil Hare. This postcard by Arnold of Market Drayton shows the church after its refit. The new chandeliers had still not been fitted in the nave.

43. In the 1860s, Sir Percival Heywood commissioned G.E.Street to design All Saints Church for the new parish of Denstone. It is notable for its rich decor, also by Street, and for three different styles of window in the nave - only two of these are visible in this 1910 postcard by H.Hansen of Ashbourne.

44. Christ Church, Knightley, is an odd-looking church with an excessively high bellcote, round headed windows and lancets growing "ears". The architect in 1841 was Thomas Trubshaw. The chancel, added in 1882, on the right in this 1905 postcard by H.Osbourne, is more normal Gothic style. The postcard was posted at Eccleshall in September, 1905.

45. St Thomas', Butterton, near Newcastle, was built by Thomas Hopper in 1844 in a Norman style. The building with its squat tower, low pyramid roof and solid round headed windows and doors looks heavy. Postcard by Charles Deakin, 1910.

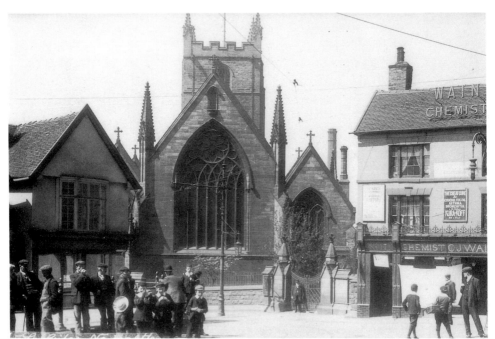

46. St Giles', Newcastle, has a medieval tower with seven-feet thick walls at the base. The rest of the church was rebuilt by Sir George Gilbert Scott in a thirteenth century style. The postcard is by William Blake, 1907.

47. St Mary's, shown on this 1905 Meacham postcard, is the third church on this Market Square site in Lichfield. Tower and spire are by G.E.Street, the rest of the building by James Fowler. It was consecrated in 1870 as a memorial to a previous vicar, Henry Lonsdale. Since 1981 the church has been a heritage centre.

48. Bethesda in Albion Street, Hanley, was built by the Methodist New Connexion in 1819. In 1859 the congregation gave their chapel the imposing facade with Corinthian pillars and a central Venetian window shown on this 1910 postcard by James Jervis of Hanley.

49. Tunstall was at the heart of Primitive Methodism. This "Sun" series postcard, produced to mark the centenary of the movement, shows the front added to the chapel in Tunstall in 1860. The building was closed in 1971 when several Methodist churches were amalgamated.

50. The huge smoke-blackened Wesleyan Chapel at Swan Bank, Burslem, seen in this 1905 Valentine postcard, reveals the importance of Methodism in the Pottery towns. The original brick building of 1801 was enlarged in 1870 when it was given this massive classical front. In 1971 the chapel was replaced by the present Mission building. The card was posted from Burslem to Ivybridge in March 1907.

51. The Wesleyan Chapel, Burslem, would seat 1200 people. The style of the building reminds you of eighteenth century churches like Burton-on-Trent (No.29). The central organ, with space for the choir below it, also reminds you of the musical tradition of these churches. T.C.series postcard, 1927, published for Vaughan of Burslem.

52. The Wesleyan Chapel, Bignall End, Audley was another huge chapel. Originally built in 1810, it was rebuilt in 1876 at a cost of £4,000 to seat 725 people. The size of these chapels and the hard work needed to raise money for them was a source of pride to their congregations. Postcard by William Shaw, 1905.

53. The Wesleyan Methodist Temple in Victoria Road, Tamworth, was built in 1877. At the topping out ceremony when it was finished, the chapel choir sang hymns from the roof and finished with a triumphant Hallelujah Chorus. In 1970 the Temple closed and the building is now used by the Victoria Club. A 1905 Stewart & Woolf postcard.

54. The Congregational Zion Chapel in Martin Street, Stafford, was built in 1811. At first it was too big and costly for its congregation but by 1896 the congregation had increased and the chapel was extended and given this baroque facade removed from Stafford General Infirmary. The chapel was demolished in 1965.

55. Not all chapels were large and costly. Harry Osbourne posed the proud congregation outside their small Primitive Methodist chapel at Woodseaves in High Offley parish for this 1905 postcard. The chapel, originally built in1863, had been carefully restored in 1887.

56. In 1907 the vicar and parishioners of St Luke's, Silverdale, raised £500 for a new peel of bells for the church. The new bells were paraded round the village by horse and cart before all the Sunday School girls were photographed with them. There is a similar postcard with the Sunday School boys.

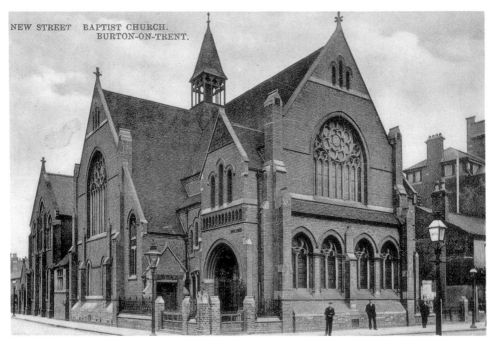

57. By the end of the nineteenth century, even nonconformist chapels had Gothic features. The Baptist Chapel on the corner of New Street, Burton-on-Trent, seen on this 1906 Jackson & Son postcard, was built in 1883 to replace an earlier building. It was destroyed by fire in 1966.

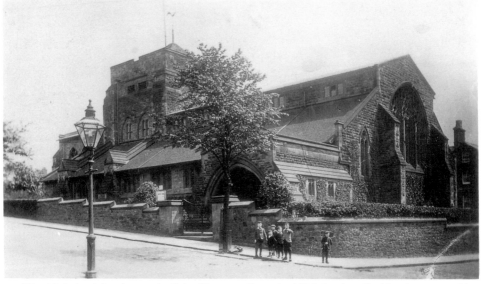

58. All Saints', Leek, was built by Norman Shaw in 1885-7 using Gothic elements with no attempt at historical consistency. Shaw described it as the best and most satisfactory piece of work he had ever done. On this W.H.Smith & Son postcard of 1908, the chancel appears high because of the sloping site.

59. This simple Primitive Methodist church at Kingsley has the dates 1834-1910 over the window. 1834 was the date of first building and 1910 when it was rebuilt. The postcard, produced shortly after the rebuilding, shows Mr and Mrs Carr (on the right) and two other members of the congregation.

60. The Roman Catholic Church of the Sacred Heart at Tunstall, opened in 1930, was designed by J.S.Brocklesby and completed by Father Ryan. The building is in a style more commonly found in southern Europe, with five green domes as well as large and short towers.

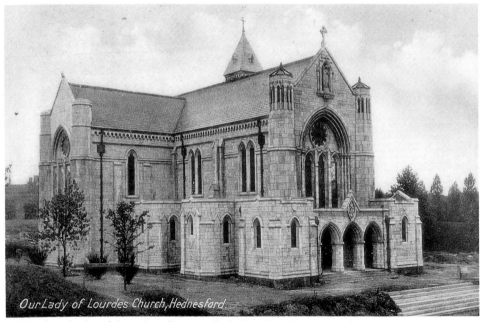

OurLady of Lourdes Church,Hednesford

61. Our Lady of Lourdes Roman Catholic Church, Hednesford, is an ambitious building that seems to have been influenced by medieval French churches. In fact it was built by G.B.Cox of Birmingham in 1927-33. This 1938 R.A.P. Co postcard clearly shows the individually projecting side chapels.